LOVE AND OTHER THOUGHTS

LOVE AND OTHER THOUGHTS

A Collection of Poems

VICTORIA E. RANKIN

Love and Other Thoughts

blue lotus press

ISBN: 099751230X
ISBN 13: 9780997512304
Library of Congress Control Number: 2016907657
Blue Lotus Press, Charlotte, NC

CONTENTS

INTRODUCTION

Writing has always been a way for me to clarify and express my thoughts. Journals, fiction, plays, poems, lyrics—all provide the means to express what I find otherwise difficult to communicate. Inspiration comes from many places. In some cases dreams inspire me, other times a person or event. Some of what I write is autobiographical; some of it has nothing to do with my personal experiences, real or imagined. But always the words resonate with me; they speak to me in a voice that often feels as if it is external to me. It is as if I am a conduit for words that emerge from a place that any of us could occupy at any given time.

This volume is a selection of poems that I wrote between 1982 and 2011. When I first considered publishing these, I organized them chronologically. Almost immediately, I realized that, although quite reflective of my thoughts and expressions as they evolved, organizing the poems that way made little sense. So I decided, at least to the extent that I could, to arrange them thematically.

The first section—*Searching*—contains poems I wrote during periods of yearning and feelings of isolation. Most of my longing had to do with love, in terms of both friendship and romance. Like most people, I enjoy having friends and lovers—and am privileged at times to find both within the same person—and sometimes experience despondency at the lack of either. And like many, I am an eternal optimist. I write about love and friends when I feel surrounded by both, as well as when I don't feel I have either. It is part of the human condition, I believe, to seek relationships with others. My writing reflects this belief.

In the next section—*Love and Friendship*—I express that particular joy that arises from knowing another. This can be found in the feeling one has upon the first encounter with a potential romantic interest, or in the shared pleasure of intimacy with a beloved, or in the ties that bind a life-long friendship. It can be found in parenting, in being part of a family, whether the bonds are by blood or by choice. Love, for me, encompasses all and everything that crosses our paths and reminds us of being alive. The ecstatic reality of being able to engage in passion—the passion of feelings, of friendship, of love, of life—is what I seek to express in this section.

The final section—*Other Thoughts*— contains poems that did not seem to fit well in the previous sections. In this segment, I share my fears, anxieties, hopes, and dreams. Topics in these poems reflect either actual experiences or recurring thoughts and images. The poems in this section, even when the subject arouses fears and anxiety, speak to positions of strength and continuity, never defeat.

Putting pen to paper, which is how I continue to capture the majority of my creative thinking, is a very personal endeavor for me. The decision to publish this volume, and thereby expose my thoughts, did not come easily. However, as I read through and selected poems for inclusion in this book, I was reminded of the emotions that accompanied each verse. Re-reading these poems led me to reflect on my growth and the difference in my current perspective or to smile at the memory of the passion that inspired them. In sharing my creative expression, I hope those who read this book are encouraged, inspired, and motivated to live fully, love deeply, and cherish each moment of life.

Victoria Elizabeth Rankin
Charlotte, NC
2016

Dedicated to my daughter, Imani, who continually inspires thoughts of love.

SEARCHING

WHERE WERE YOU?

All of these years I've been alone
Keeping it together and going on
Where were you?

When I yearned for love and someone
With whom it I could express
When I desired to be cuddled and kissed
And when I felt depressed
Where were you?

Why is it that when I needed a friend
You couldn't be found?
What kept you so occupied
That you weren't around?
But you say you were there, visible to me
I say where were you? How come I didn't see?

Were you the one who said
I was too fat, too ugly, with not enough hair?
Were you the one so concerned with
The outer me you viewed
That you never took time to notice
The inner me, which is constantly renewed

With you I could not share my secrets
My joys, my sorrows, nor my hopes and fears
And I was afraid to let you see me shed my tears

For you were impressed by superficial things
While I sought someone with whom I could
Spread my wings

If you've now decided I meet your approval
Don't come to me
If you've considered letting me in your circle
Don't come to me
If you've concluded that I can be of value to you
Don't come to me; leave me be
When I needed a friend
Through thick and thin
Where were you?

BLACK MAN

Speak to me from your wisdom
Touch me where I hurt
Extend your inner-self to me
Make me turn inside out
Black man

Don't fight me
For I am a part of you
As I respect you, respect me
Love me from way down
Deep, deep
Beyond the surface
Deep, deep

Like a cool drink of water
Quench my thirst
My thirst for love, for life, for you
Like a full meal
Satisfy my hunger
My hunger for love, for life, for you
Like a fire
Which can warm a cold day
Warm my feelings and let them flow
For love, for life, for you
Black man

IN SEARCH OF LOVE

We speak in plaintive voices
Hoping someone will hear
We cry with silent shouting
Wishing someone was near

Afraid to show vulnerability
We front a façade that's strong
Terrified of how we're judged
We stifle our own song

We grab ahold of flotsam
Lacking a helping hand
And receive from that as much support
As a deep pit of quicksand

Intimate love with another
We think has been denied
No one was there to wipe away
The lonely tears we cried

But through the mist and foggy surface
Through the winds of storms that rage
A Lover beckons us
As It has in every age

If we would just catch Its flight
On eagles' wings we'd soar

If we would just listen in the still of the night
We'd hear Its mighty roar

This is the Love that fulfills us
When all else seems veiled behind a curtain
This is the Comforter that abides
Even when Its presence seems uncertain
And when this Love that exceeds all others
Is recognized and accorded Its due
Then the presence or absence of others
Takes on a different tone, another hue

And when things eternal are seen
The temporal is in its place
We understand our journey through this world
And acknowledge the Creator's grace

DESPAIR

Eyes swollen shut by tears of despair
Heartstrings straining for something not there

Misery for company, feeling all alone
Hope dissolved for consolation
Through the telephone

Reaching in for strength hidden
Giving up on external love
That begins to seem forbidden

Finding what's needed to carry on
For in addition to myself
Another has been born

So, let the well run dry and wipe away the tears
Though the night seemed full of sorrow
A new sun sheds light on old fears

And though my heart, still heavy with despair
Feels burdened by existence
Another thought enters here

If love from another is not meant to be
Then I should use my time
Learning to love me

LOVE AND FRIENDSHIP

FOR ELLEN

Though you say
You look in a mirror
To remind yourself to keep going
And though you say
You feel worthless
It's not true

In you is the spirit
Which creates the songs
The rest of us sing

In you are the words
To the story
The rest of us read

You hold the melody
To which we dance

So

Be of good courage
And hold your head high
For in you the rest of us live
Without your spirit
We don't survive

SELF-CONTAINED

Self-contained
In my own place and in my own space
Heart beating in my body
Blood running through my veins

Self-contained
My madness, my sickness, my hurt
My agony, my tears, my pain

Self-contained
All that I need I have
All that I will be I am
Emotions are mine to give
Love, laughter, the life I live
In control of my world, I am

Self-contained
Sharing is my choice
When I speak, it is my voice
If I do not listen, no one will hear
You cannot come close unless I draw you near, I am

Self-contained
Me, myself and I; my trinity
Holy wars fought against my ego
Best friend, worst enemy, I am
Self-contained

But wait...

What is this I feel inside?
What is this I've been careful to hide?
A capacity to love someone other than myself
A williness to give for the comfort of someone else
To communicate, invigorate,
Embrace with grace
Imbue by divine command,
Support, uphold, understand

So it is, in the midst of being
Self-contained
I discover what I have known all along:
A part of me is
You

TO MY SISTERS

They will cut off your feet
So that you can no longer walk or run
Or skip through fields of lilies

They will chop you off at the knees
To cut you down to size
And ensure that you cannot stand the taller

They will break you at the hip
Too ample, too much like a woman
A constant reminder of where they've passed through

They will sear your belly with a hot iron
An attempt to burn shame into your flesh
And leave a mark of domination

They will laugh at your breasts
Criticize them as too large, too small
Forgetting that it was your breasts
From which the world first fed

They will nibble at your fingers
Rob you of your means of self-expression
Dare you to point the way for others

They will shatter your arms
Render you unable to hug somebody

The way you yearn to be hugged

They will eat your ears, bite off your nose, rip out your tongue
Lest you smell the fragrance of life, hear the songs of God
And sing them to another

They would just as soon decapitate you
Rather than let you think

Most of all, they will utterly destroy your heart
Believing it to be connected to your soul
Which you are not supposed to have

But, oh, my sisters
Don't you let them!

Step firmly with your feet and stand tall
Sway your hips and let your belly shake
Thrust out your breasts, as you extend your fingers
Using the power of your arms
To embrace the world

And breathe, sisters, breathe!
The sweet perfume of life
Listen to the voices of wisdom
That have gone before and will follow after

And sing your song
For through the words
Of your unique melody
We gather our strength

LESSON

If you were all that mattered
Then I would feel defeat
If yours was the only love
This would be time for retreat

If your version of life
Were the only one that's true
Then my existence would be meaningless
Without the presence of you

But because I have my own story
Because there are chapters in my book
Your ideas don't go unchallenged
I can take a second look

I matter just as much as you
And maybe even more
Yours is not the only love
You were just one door

There are many others
And now I've found the key
The way to unlock my happiness
Is to learn how to love me

LOVE IS

Love is like a rose
Trying to bloom in the middle of winter
Its edges are wilted with frost
But it shares a sweet-smelling scent
With those brave enough to come close

Love is like a full moon
Dark and foreboding on one side
But brilliantly illuminated on the other
For those who dare to take a look

Love is like a seed
Hard to the touch and tightly encased
But yielding forth fruit gladly
When tended with the proper care

Love is like the written word
Indecipherable to the unlearned
But absolute magic
For those who can read

Love is like water
Powerful enough to destroy
But the elixir of life
Without which death will quickly come

Love is like a star
Waiting to be discovered
Before it implodes upon itself
And leaves a black hole
Where light used to be

BURNING

We strike our minds
And light a fire
Whose warmth has spread
From our head to our loins

Whether typing, talking
Visualizing what might be
Making plans to consummate
A date with destiny

Does it seem odd
That our paths should cross?
Or the appearance
Of obstacles in the way?

Not to me since I believe
This want, this need
Shall be satisfied
Come what may

Miles separate us
But fortune has allowed
Us to find one another
Some way, some how

JOINING

The meeting of our minds
Render the melding of our bodies
A greater possibility

The words we speak
Allow us to contemplate other uses
For our lips

The visions we create
Will enable us to enjoy
The beings that we are

But until we've closed the distance
Passion remains a mystery
The burning, the yearning,
The longing to have you beside me

So, make haste, my friend
And travel with due speed
So we may as lovers
Joined be

And through our ecstasy
Be as two souls
In a meeting of body and mind
Joined as a complimentary whole

INSPIRATION

I think of you and my heart sings songs
And I compose poetry in my head

Melodies linger, words whisper
In rhythms I have not yet read

I hear the devotions of times long gone
Through which many have already passed

I see glimpses of future connotations
The hope for which love lasts

When I think of you my spirit rises
In recognition

Of a kindred one who finds himself
In similar condition

I think of you and take a deep breath
And feel the tingling in my skin

As your essence is mixed with mine
Then I exhale again

If my words would capture emotions
And allow the repeated sensation

They'd remind me whenever I think of you
My soul sighs "Inspiration!"

FRIENDSHIP

Imagine conversations
From a chance meeting in cyberspace
Leading to unplanned interaction
In a very confined place
Makes for lasting first impressions
Reminds me of life's enduring lessons

That you never know where friends will be found
Or with whom you'll find common ground
Or who will bring joy and laughter
With passionate pleasure, emotion-filled ever after

Where will it lead? How long will it last?
Who can tell the future
When we hardly know the past?
So let's take each day one moment at a time
Share our good feelings like a bottle of fine wine

Let's cherish this newly discovered
Relationship
And nourish, to full bloom, our budding
Friendship

KINDRED

Elongated
Stretches of time
Alone with myself
Introspective, reflective

Lonely? Sometimes
More often engaged
In the company of
My solitude

There I heard whispers
Dreamed visions
Nourished hope
That I would encounter
Another

Fine mind
Sharp, quick, courageous
Keeping time to a different
Rhythm

Finally, again, our paths crossed
Who knew that the route I traveled
Would take me back
Full circle to
You?

RECOGNIZED

When we were young I didn't recognize your value
Or appreciate your worth
I thought men like you were a dime a dozen
Now I know better

Courage is hard to find in others who hide
Behind the façade of bravado
Authenticity is difficult to see in those who insist
On being who they are not

Intellectualism is found in many
But emotional intelligence, kindness,
Consideration, and gentleness are found in few

Respect, oh, yes—respect
I've never met a man who showed so much
And treated me like that which I am
A precious gift
To be loved, valued, honored, not taken for granted

You were the gift the universe brought to me
But I couldn't see then what I've since learned
Through hard lessons and my own growth

That a man like you, once found, must be
Kept. Honored. Respected. Loved.

FALLING IN LOVE

I look inside myself and see
Deconstructed, but identifiable
Change in me

Hormones shifting
Chemical interactions
I'd almost forgotten
The power of attraction

Your voice in my ear
Hours passing in the night
Takes me back to a time
Before I took flight

I flew away from you
When I should have stayed
I didn't understand then
The qualities you displayed

Now I return to you
Like a trained dove
This time I descend
A woman
Falling in love

OTHER THOUGHTS

NEW HORIZON

Through the shimmering curtain
Of dawn
I see myself
On a new horizon

Looking down
The precipice
Up from whence
I've soared

Looking ahead
To a new beginning
More comfortable
Being myself

Liking the skin I'm in
Acknowledging the gifts I have
Grateful to Spirit
For the life I lead

LET ME BE ME

Let me be
Me
Cute!
With my broad hips
And small breasts
With my flat feet
And thick lips
Cute!

Let me be
Me
With my pigeon toes
And my knocked-knees
With my flabby arms
And my nappy hair

Let me be
Me
Cute!
With the strength of my ancestors
And the spirit of women
Who in all shapes and sizes
And colors and attitudes and vibrations
Have passed through this struggle
Before me

I am fine!

Just
Let
Me
Be
Me

LIFE ON HOLD

Life on hold
Is like a breath
Waiting to be inhaled
Dreams deferred
Hopes put aside
Moving in the direction
Of limitations we set

Life on hold
Is like a song
Yet to be sung
Notes caught in a throat
Too constricted to open
Constrained by memories
Of someone else's pain

But what if we dare to live
Reaching beyond our boundaries
Stretching our wings
To soar through space
Heretofore unimagined?

What if you sing
A song of your own
Adding your unique melody
To the harmony of the world?

What if you gave energy
To fulfilling your dreams
As if they were the foundation
Of your reality?

What if you contemplated
The potential of our being and then acted as if
Your very existence depended upon it?

For a life not fully lived is
Life on hold

NO

I said "no," but you didn't hear me
No, you can't make my decisions for me
Or compel me to ride your emotional rollercoaster
I said "no."

No, you can't make me love you
Or even pretend I like you
Or surrender to you
The choices for my life
I said "no."

No, I will not have you as a lover
I reserve my right to select
I may not have you as a friend
If you remain persistently hard of hearing
I said "no."

Do you know how it feels to not be heard?
Like trying to scream
With your mouth sealed shut
Or needing to breathe while deep under water
Like you will explode from the frustration
Of constant, unrelenting, miscommunication
I said "no."

Apparently, what I say does not matter
My words, like so many beads of sweat upon your brow

Are wiped away by the back of your hand
They strike no responsive chord in you
Of another person's right to choose

So I shout, act out
Erect emotional barriers
Make you think I am insane
You call me out of my name
Wonder why I act so strange
And when you ask again
My reply will remain:
I said "no!"

ON THE TABLE

Many, many men standing around
All Caucasian (it appears), looking down
I'm on the table, name unknown
They're here to remove that which was my own

Symbolic of my 'femaleness', epitome of the woman in me
The vessel through which my only child was birthed
The means through which the world was populated; what is it worth?

It is dis-eased, I've been told
It is not at peace, I feel
And after seven opinions I've decided
To lay its agony still

But I did not know there would only be men in this room with me
I'd no idea there would not be any women, at least none that I could see
And so, on this day, when a part of me is lost
It is men, once again, who extract the cost
Men in high positions, that I must rely on
Men who without the likes of me would not have been born

But even as it is a man who surgically removes my uterus
Leaving me free of pain
I acknowledge that it will be with a man
That I reclaim that part of myself, again

WOMAN

Sitting here considering
Myself as a woman
Am I too strong?
Have I been too meek?
Should I speak only when spoken to?
Or vocalize even if unasked?

Other women tell me
"It's a balancing act;
Be smart, be bold, but don't let men know"
The men tell me
I'm perceived as a threat
"Earn a salary, carry some weight,
But don't mess with my ego"

My professional life
Is not what I want it to be
Not aggressive, too aggressive
I've been accused of both
My personal life
Is not what I want it to be
Not soft enough, so soft almost foolish
I've been accused of both

Now I have a daughter to whom I'd like to pass
Lessons I've learned about being
A woman:

Daughter, when you're told
You're too strong
Remember
It was the strength of women
That helped carry the human race forward

And when they say
You're too meek
Remember
It was meekness
That saved many lives

And when do you speak?
My dear, you speak
Whenever you have something to say

For sisters who tell you
It's a balancing act
Remember
Your only charge is to be the best
Of your highest potential

And, darling, for the brothers
Who say you threaten their ego
Remember
The only ego you can control
Is your own

So, what is a woman?
A woman is all of these things
Or any of them

At different times
The only constant is
A woman
Is who she must
Be
Imbued by Spirit
Not bound by gender

To my daughter
And all the women in the world:
Reach in to find who you really are
Simultaneously, reach out
Touch the stars
After all
You helped hang them there
As a
Woman

VOICE

Yearning to speak freely
But silent so long
Stopped my introspection
Is that what was wrong?

I used to talk a lot
Too much, some would say
My words could not be suppressed
Their life, their emotion, their way

But then, I forgot to honor myself
Internalizing the reactions of others
Their baggage is not mine
Those so-called sisters and brothers

And so silence came
Even in the still of the night
Communication ceased
Of my spirit, I lost sight

But now, I've learned again
Where my strength resides
To acknowledge my Creator
From whom none can hide

And when least expected
Without fanfare or choice

A spontaneous reconnection
To the power of my voice

I speak more discriminately
With more wisdom than before
I speak with more authority
At the threshold of my soul's door

My being-ness surrounds me
In self-reflection I rejoice
And once again, pen to paper
I've found my voice